SPIDERS AND DADDY LONG LEGS

BY MEGAN GENDELL

The Child's World®
childsworld.com

Published by The Child's World®
1980 Lookout Drive • Mankato, MN 56003-1705
800-599-READ • www.childsworld.com

Photographs ©: Vova Shevchuk/Shutterstock Images, cover (spider), 2, 11, 20, 24 (spider); Melinda Fawver/Shutterstock Images, cover (daddy long legs), 2–3, 15, 21, 24 (daddy long legs); iStockphoto, 5, 17; Shutterstock Images, 6; Cathy Keifer/Shutterstock Images, 9; Corey Tackett/Shutterstock Images, 10; Chartcharn Phodhiphad/Shutterstock Images, 13; Bruce MacQueen/Shutterstock Images, 14; Federico Crovetto/Shutterstock Images, 19

ISBN 9781503835856
LCCN 2019943001

Printed in the United States of America

ABOUT THE AUTHOR

Megan Gendell is a writer and editor. She lives in Philadelphia. She shares her home with two cats, four people, and many spiders.

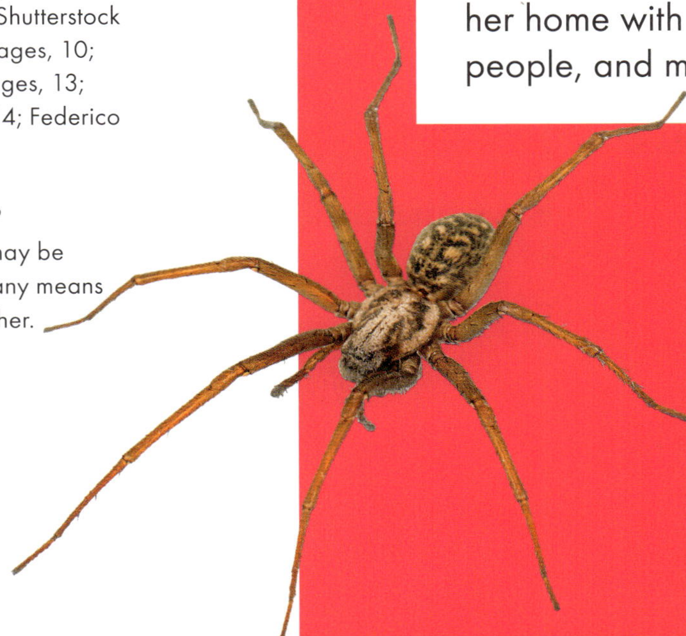

TABLE OF CONTENTS

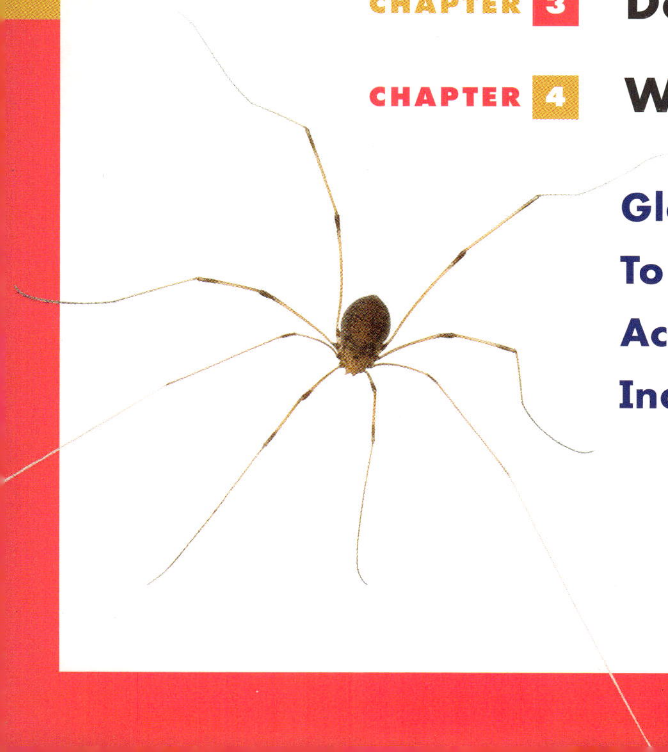

CHAPTER

1

Eight Legs

An eight-legged creature crawls up an old tree trunk. It eats insects. Is it a spider or a daddy long legs? What's the difference?

Spiders are found on every continent except Antarctica.

The strands of a spiderweb are thinner than a human hair!

CHAPTER 2

Spiders

A spider has eight legs. Its body has two parts. The legs connect to the front part. A spider's mouth and eyes are also on the front. Most spiders have eight eyes. The back of the body makes webs.

Spiders make **silk** and weave it into webs. The webs catch insects. Spiders bite and eat the insects they catch. Spiders' **fangs** have a poison called **venom**. Venom helps spiders trap their **prey**. They eat insects that may bother people. Most spiders can't bite people. Their fangs are too small to go through skin.

Spiderwebs are very sticky, making it hard for prey to escape.

Spiders can regrow many legs.

Sometimes a spider loses a leg. A **predator** might grab the leg. The leg falls off, and the spider escapes. Spiders can regrow lost legs later.

CHAPTER 3

Daddy Long Legs

Daddy long legs are also called harvestmen. Their bodies are small and round. Their bodies have two parts, but they are stuck together like one piece. Daddy long legs have eight legs. The legs are very long and thin. Daddy long legs have two eyes.

The legs of most daddy long legs are several times longer than their bodies.

Some types of daddy long legs gather in groups.

Daddy long legs cannot make silk or weave webs. Daddy long legs eat tiny insects and dead plants. They do not have fangs. And they do not have venom. They cannot hurt people.

A daddy long legs can live if a leg comes off. A predator might catch one leg. The daddy long legs can run away without that leg. The leg can **twitch** by itself! The predator might pay attention to the leg. The daddy long legs escapes, but the leg does not grow back.

A daddy long legs can still move easily after losing more than one leg.

CHAPTER 4

What's the Difference?

Spiders and daddy long legs both have eight legs. But daddy long legs have longer, thinner legs than most spiders. A spider's body has two parts. The body of a daddy long legs looks like one round piece.

Both spiders and daddy long legs are arachnids, or bugs with eight legs.

Most spiders have eight eyes. Daddy long legs have two. Spiders spin webs. Daddy long legs cannot. Most spiders have venom. Daddy long legs do not.

Both animals live all over the world. They can seem scary. But most cannot hurt people!

SPIDERS

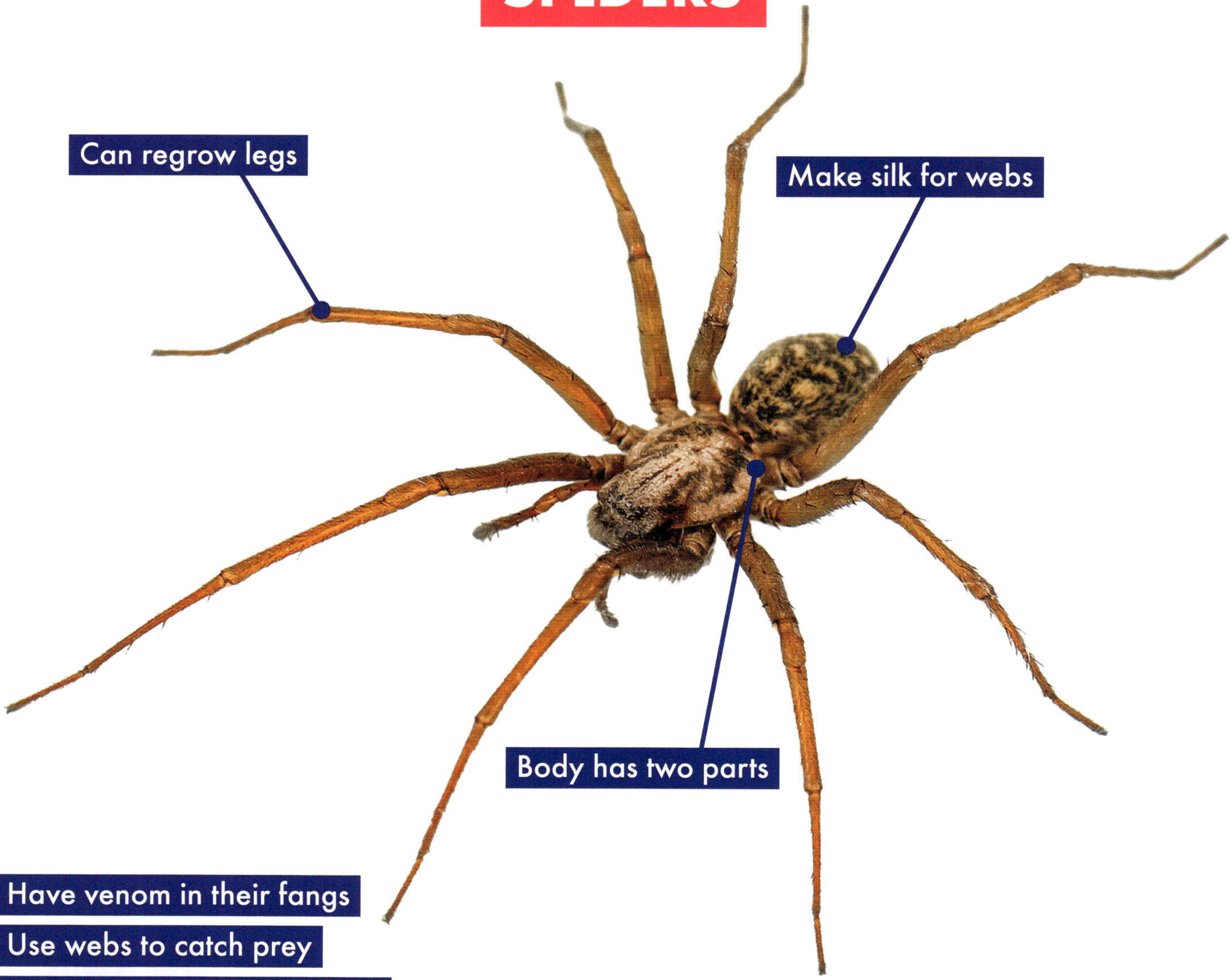

- Have venom in their fangs
- Use webs to catch prey
- Legs regrow after falling off.

DADDY LONG LEGS

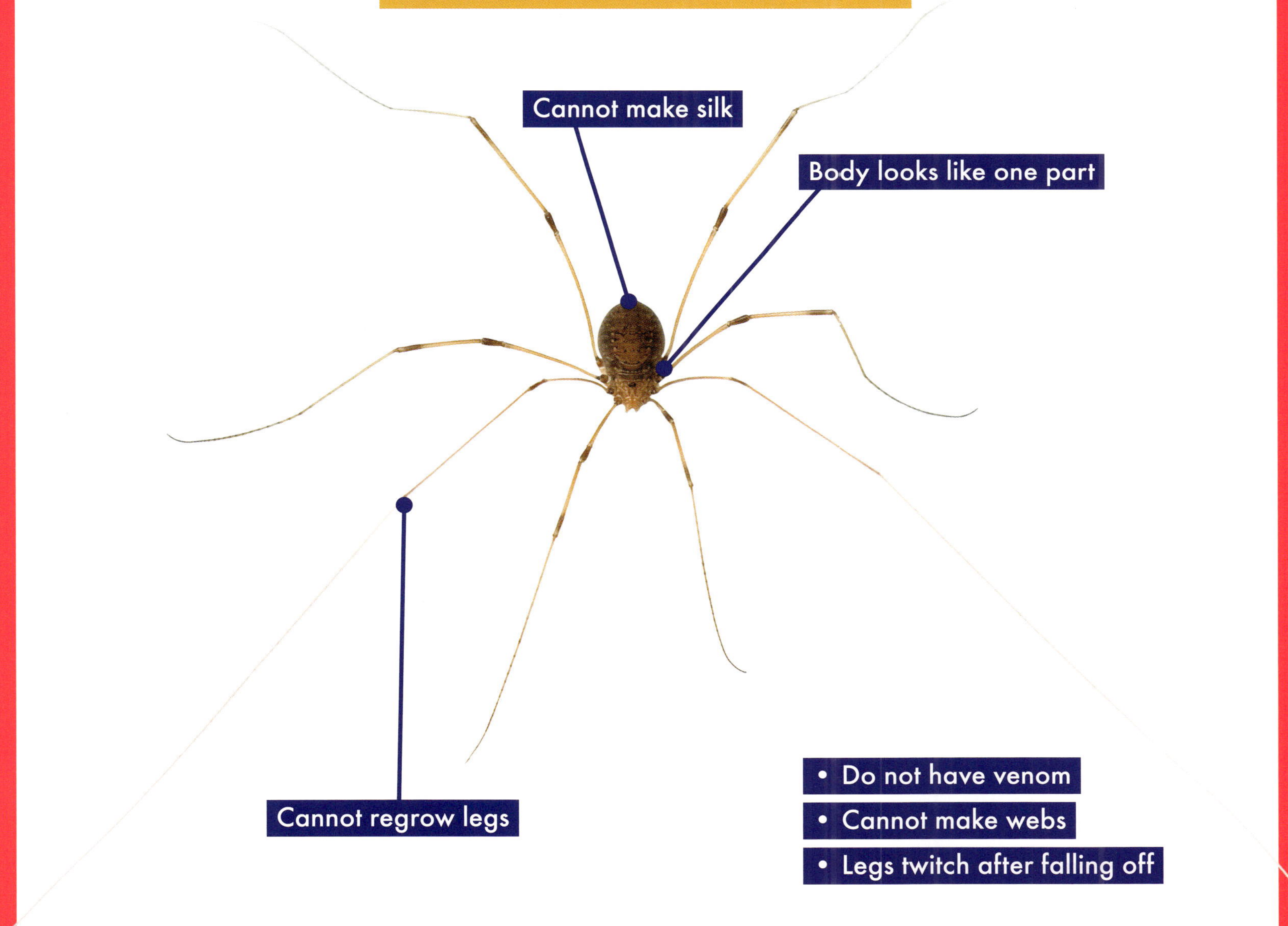

GLOSSARY

fangs (FANGZ) Fangs are long, sharp teeth. Spiders bite their food with their fangs.

predator (PREH-duh-tor) A predator is an animal that hunts and eats another animal. A daddy long legs can be caught by a predator.

prey (PRAY) Prey are animals that are eaten by other animals. Spiders use venom to catch their prey.

silk (SILK) Silk is a thread that spiders make. Spiders use silk to make webs.

twitch (TWITCH) To twitch is to make small, fast movements. A leg that comes off a daddy long legs can twitch.

venom (VEN-om) Venom is a poison that an animal makes to hurt or kill another animal. Spiders have venom in their fangs.

TO LEARN MORE

IN THE LIBRARY

Guyton, John W. *Bug Lab for Kids*. Beverly, MA: Quarry Books, 2018.

Patterson, Jack. *Spiders*. New York, NY: Cavendish Square, 2019.

Sharif, Meghan. *Why Do Wolf Spiders Make Burrows? And Other Odd Arachnid Adaptations*. New York, NY: Gareth Stevens Publishing, 2019.

ON THE WEB

Visit our website for links about spiders and daddy long legs:

childsworld.com/links

Note to Parents, Teachers, and Librarians: We routinely verify our Web links to make sure they are safe and active sites. So encourage your readers to check them out!

ACTIVITY

Draw a picture of a spider and a daddy long legs. Your picture should clearly show the differences between the spider and the daddy long legs. Look at pages 20 and 21 for help.

INDEX